Encyclopedias Brown and White

Encyclopedias Brown and White

A FoxTrot Collection by Bill Amend

Andrews McMeel
Publishing

Kansas City

FoxTrot is distributed internationally by Universal Press Syndicate.

Encyclopedias Brown and White copyright © 2001 by Bill Amend. All rights reserved. Printed in the United States of America. No part of this book may be used or reproduced in any manner whatsoever without written permission except in the case of reprints in the context of reviews. For information, write Andrews McMeel Publishing, 4520 Main Street, Kansas City, Missouri 64111.

01 02 03 04 05 BAH 10 9 8 7 6 5 4 3 2

ISBN: 0-7407-1850-9

Library of Congress Catalog Card Number: 2001088686

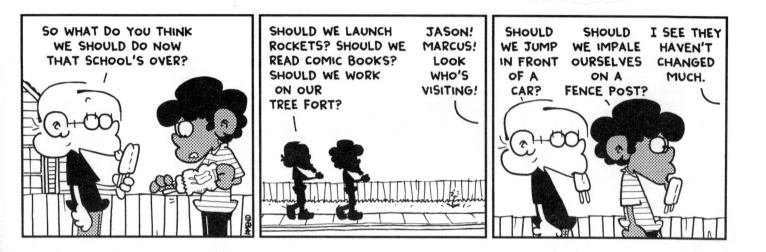

26

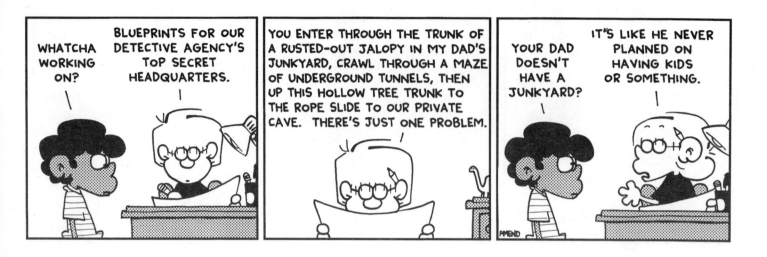

29

31

47

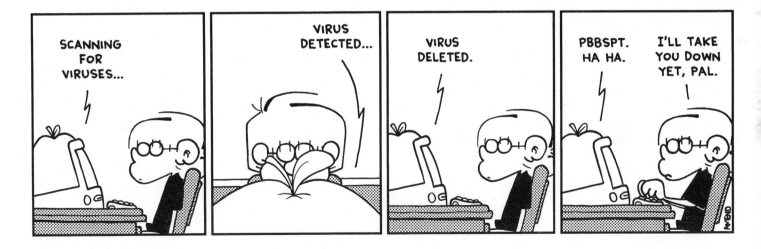

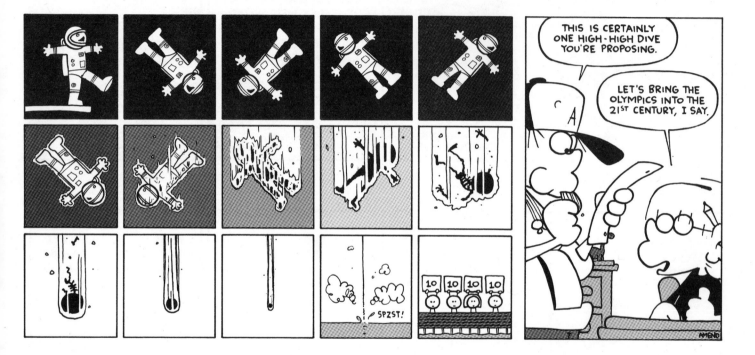

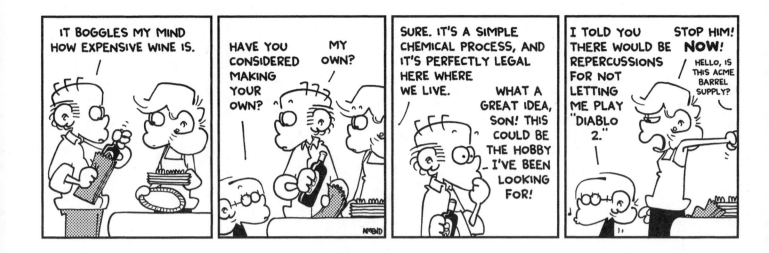

60

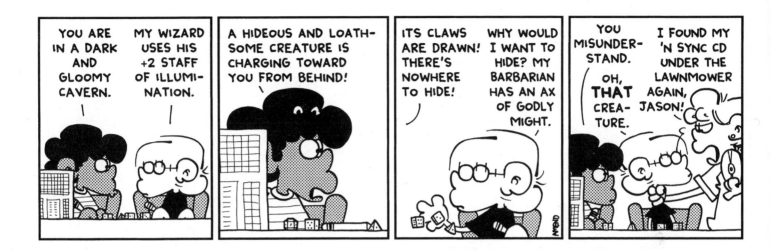

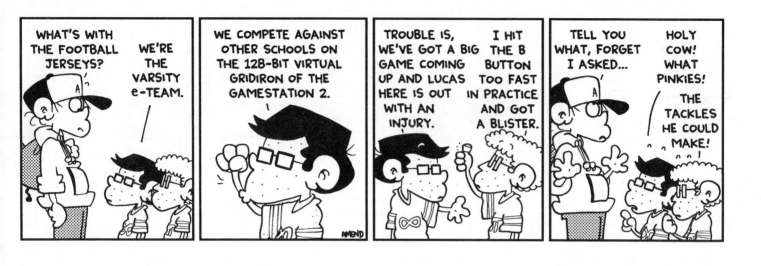

74

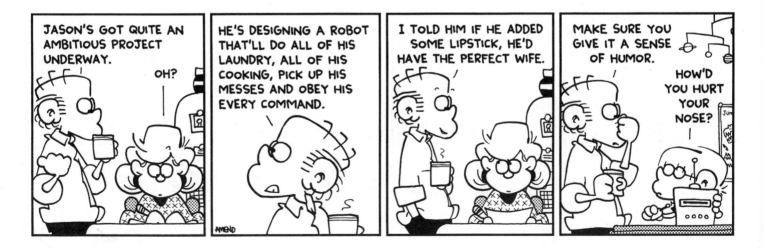

83

90

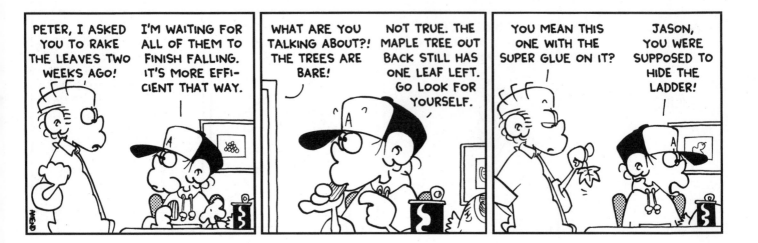

It was even more luxurious than the first one.

Twice as long. Four times as many passengers.

They called it the ship that this time really couldn't go wrong.

But then...

Every soul but one plunged into the dark icy water that sad, sad day.

TITANIC II

THE TRAGEDY CONTINUES

A Jason Fox Mega-Blockbuster Script

109

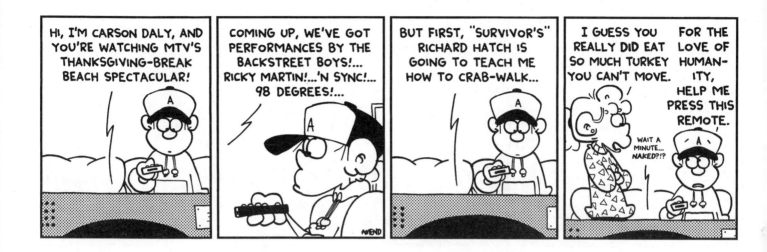

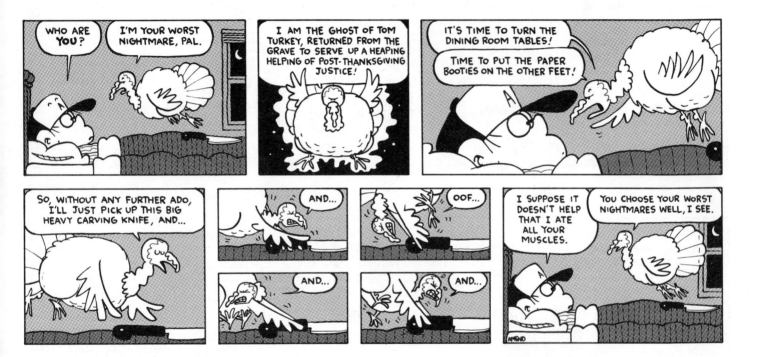

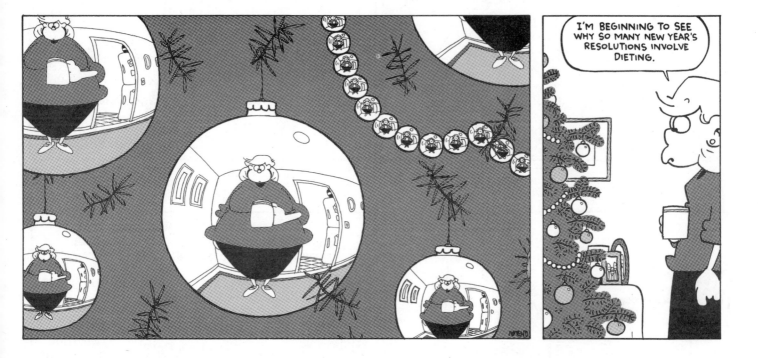

117